SIBELIUS
THE SYMPHONIES

SIBELIUS
THE SYMPHONIES

BY
CECIL GRAY

 BOOKS FOR LIBRARIES PRESS
FREEPORT, NEW YORK

First Published 1935
Reprinted 1970

MT
130
S5
G7
1970

STANDARD BOOK NUMBER:
8369-5283-9

LIBRARY OF CONGRESS CATALOG CARD NUMBER:
78-114879

*

PRINTED IN THE UNITED STATES OF AMERICA

PREFACE

In a recent monograph on Sibelius the present writer, partly for reasons of space, partly because of the absence of musical illustrations, was unable to do more than give a highly generalized survey of the symphonies, with only short and necessarily inadequate descriptions of each of them individually. Since that book was published, in 1931, these works have gradually established themselves in the repertory of every important orchestra in the English-speaking world, and in view of this development it was felt that there existed a definite need for a booklet of this kind, amply provided with musical examples, which would deal with each individual symphony in a manner more analytical and expository than critical or appreciative, as in the earlier book.

At the same time, seeing that there is surely no more pathetically futile occupation in the world than to attempt to paraphrase and put into other words what one has already said elsewhere to the best of whatever ability one possesses, the writer has not scrupled to make use of occasional observations he may have happened to make in the earlier book which seemed appropriate to the different purpose of the present one. But such self-quotations are few and far between.

Finally, he has to thank Mr. Constant Lambert for pointing out the singularly close resemblance between a passage at the end of the Seventh Symphony and a progression from 'Valse triste', which is duly indicated

Preface

on page 77. Many other listeners besides oneself must have experienced the same puzzled impression of something exceedingly familiar in this passage which they were unable to identify, and will similarly be grateful to Mr. Lambert for having elucidated the mystery.

C. G.

ACKNOWLEDGEMENTS

For kind permission to reprint musical quotations thanks are due to the following publishers:—

Breitkopf and Härtel, Leipzig (Symphonies Nos. 1, 2, and 4).

Schlesinger'sche Musik und Buchhandlung, Berlin (Symphony No. 3).

Wilhelm Hansen, Copenhagen (Symphonies Nos. 5 and 7).

A. Hirsch Forlag, Stockholm (Symphony No. 6).

CONTENTS

Symphony No. *1*, *in* E *minor*, Op. *39*

SYMPHONY, even in its most ordinary and conventional aspect, in the form of the customary four movements consecrated by classical usage—the first with its intricate plot and predominantly intellectual appeal; the second, generally of a lyrical, subjective, and expressive order; the third, essentially a dance movement of some kind or other; the fourth, broad, epic, heroic in character—symphony is a compendium and epitome of all musical forms and styles and modes of thought. Hence it is that symphony constitutes the most formidable and searching all-round test of musicianship that could possibly be devised. Consequently it is not surprising to find that none of the outstanding landmarks in the history of the form has been created early in the life of any composer, with the possible exception of Mozart— the exception to every rule. Beethoven was thirty, Brahms forty, Elgar fifty, and César Franck sixty, before they respectively brought themselves to make their first attempts, and none of the early specimens by Haydn, Schubert, Mendelssohn, or Schumann is of primary importance, or in any way comparable to their achievements in other directions at the same stage of their various careers.

Sibelius is one of those composers who wisely refrained from measuring their strength with the symphony until they had arrived at maturity. His first attempt was made at the age of thirty-four, after he had already attained to complete mastery in other forms.

Without intruding unduly on the domain of aesthetic criticism, for which this is not the proper place, it can be said that Sibelius's First Symphony is the last of an old line rather than the first of a new. In this respect it is symbolically significant that it should have been written in the last year of the nineteenth century. Although it is true to say that no one else could have written it, the work reveals distinct affinities, both formal and colouristic, with what one may call the romantic symphonies of various predecessors and contemporaries from Dvořák to Elgar.

It consists of the regular four movements of the orthodox tradition, and it is scored for the ordinary-sized full orchestra, with two flutes, oboes, clarinets, and bassoons, four horns, three trumpets, three trombones, bass tuba, harp, and the usual strings. The percussion includes bass drum, cymbals, and triangle in addition to the kettle-drums.

First Movement: *andante ma non troppo—allegro energico.*

The work begins with a striking introduction, consisting of a finely shaped, expressive melody of elegiac character, twenty-eight bars long, in common time, sung by a solo clarinet over a soft drum-roll for the first half of its course, and entirely unaccompanied for the second. It plays no part, however, in the subsequent developments of the movement proper,

Ex. 1.

poco forte.

an *allegro* in six-four time, which begins with the
lithe, springing, vigorous, first subject announced by
the first violins, at first in octaves, and later in unison,
and imitated by the 'cellos and violas, also in octaves.
(Example 1.)

A subsidiary theme with a characteristic and strongly
marked rhythm then follows in the wood-wind and
horns, and is continued in the strings:

Ex. 2.

after which brilliant rushing scale passages lead back
to the restatement of the first subject, this time for
full orchestra. The second subject is also bi-partite,
consisting, firstly, of a figure in thirds for flutes to an
accompaniment of harps and strings:

Ex. 3.

leading to an expressive lyrical subject given out first
by an oboe solo and answered by flutes and clarinets in
four octaves against a background of syncopated string
harmonies;

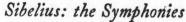

This tranquil, sunlit episode is gradually and almost imperceptibly merged into a wild, whirling dance punctuated with explosive accents, by means of a cunningly contrived *crescendo* and *accelerando* combined. Wagner said truly that the secret of composition was the art of transition, and it would be difficult to find a finer example of this difficult art of transition than is afforded by this passage, which concludes the exposition.

The development begins with a somewhat rhetorical, almost Lisztian, passage, with held chords for the heavy brass, furious downward chromatic scales for the strings, and a kind of fanfare for the wood-wind doubled in five octaves. The 'working-out', apart from one single fragmentary reference to Example 1, is almost exclusively occupied with the two constituent elements of the second subject, but especially Example 3, until we come to a passage in which slow-descending chromatics in the wood-wind (in crotchets) are set against quickly ascending chromatics for the lower strings (in quavers), upon which design is subsequently superimposed the subsidiary first subject (Example 2). This latter gradually establishes its ascendancy, and drives the chromatic scales out before it, just as the wind and the sun dispel the mists and fog of early morning. The flying scale passages of the exposition reappear, heralding the inevitable, triumphant, long-awaited recurrence of the first subject, delivered by the full orchestra—a climax all the more impressive because the psychological need for this return has become so acute that its advent has in it something of a physical relief, almost, so long has it been withheld.

The rest of the movement is a more or less regular recapitulation, though with different scoring from that of the exposition. The concluding bars are arresting —held notes for basses, divided 'cellos doubled by bassoons, a roll on the kettle-drums, all triple *forte*, and nothing else: followed by two abrupt *pizzicato* chords for upper strings and harp.

Second Movement: *andante (ma non troppo lento)*.

The slow movement begins straight away with the principal subject, a suave *cantabile* for violins doubled by 'cellos in the octave below, each clause of which is rounded off, as it were, by a little phrase for the clarinets: to an accompaniment of low horn harmonies and a tonic pedal for double basses and harp:

Ex. 5.

Con sord. semplice.

Violins. *pp*

A second strain, marked *deciso*, and confided princi-
pally to the wood-wind, is suddenly abandoned after
eight bars, and is succeeded by a somewhat contra-
puntal section—a feature of somewhat rare incidence
in the music, and more particularly the symphonies, of
Sibelius—in which the leisurely pace is set by a dialogue
between the two bassoons. Another figure based upon
the same rhythm as the opening bar of the chief subject
is introduced and is also treated contrapuntally, in
canon, by the strings, and after a passing reference back
to the main subject on the part of a solo 'cello, a middle

Ex. 6.

section, *molto tranquillo*, introduces an entirely new theme, announced by the first horn to a murmuring accompaniment of violins and harp, and harmonies for the other horns.

This section is of short duration, however. The first subject returns on the strings, but encounters unexpectedly rough treatment—a long-sustained grumble from the drums, querulous chatterings from the woodwind, and menacing gestures from the brass. As if infected by the general ill humour, the strings abandon the graceful, lyrical theme, and take part in the general mêlée, which is worked up to a high pitch of intensity. It all dies down suddenly, however, and the principal subject resumes its discourse once more, as if nothing had happened, bringing the movement to a tranquil and peaceful close.

Third Movement: *scherzo (allegro)*.

Over a thrummed *pizzicato* accompaniment for violas and 'cellos, the violins, anticipated by the kettle-drums, give out the first phrase of the subject, to which the wood-wind and horns make reply—a rough, jovial theme of a distinctly Beethovenian cast, which is, moreover, accentuated by the treatment to which it is subjected:

A second motive which plays an important role in the movement is:

Ex. 8.

Flute *mp.*

Highly ingenious and anticipatory of the composer's later symphonic style is the, way in which the two subjects are merged into one in a kind of *fugato* passage which begins in the wood-wind:

Ex. 9.

Flute 8*va.*

In the *trio*, as in the *scherzo* proper, wood-wind maintains precedence over the strings; the pipes of Pan dominate the lyre of Apollo. The atmosphere throughout is pastoral, sylvan, bucolic even.

Fourth Movement: *finale (quasi una fantasia): andante —allegro molto—andante assai.*

The *finale* begins in the same way as the first movement, with the same introductory theme, entrusted this time to the strings, and punctuated by harmonies in the brass. As in the first movement this theme plays no subsequent part in the developments. It breaks off abruptly, and is succeeded by a disjointed series of little melodic wisps and fragments, and the *tempo* fluctuates uneasily and irresolutely before finally settling down to a grim, purposeful *allegro molto,* in which several brief but pregnant and vital themes make their appearance.

Of these the most important are:

Ex. 10.

Clarinets.

Clarinets and Oboes.

Ex. 11.

'Cellos.

Ex. 12.

In striking contrast to the comparative brevity and fragmentariness of the foregoing material is the grandiose, large-scale second subject, *andante cantabile ed espressivo* for the entire massed violins playing on the G string:

Ex. 13.

At the conclusion of its presentation the *tempo* changes back to the earlier *allegro*, and Examples 10 and 11 are strenuously worked out, beginning with an elaborate kind of *fugato* based chiefly upon the former of the two. After this has been developed to a great pitch of intensity, the proceedings are clinched by the emphatic utterance of the third member of the thematic triumvirate which together constitute the first subject of the movement—Example 12. A rapid *diminuendo* takes place, and the second subject is resumed at greater length, and with an enhanced wealth of instrumental colour and volume, first by a solo clarinet, then by the strings. This is worked up to a majestic peroration for the heavy brass, and the movement concludes with fragmentary references to the foregoing material, culminating in a violent triple *forte* statement of Example 12. The actual end, however, is unexpected, coming as it does after such violent and stormy developments—two *pizzicato* chords for strings alone, the first *mezzo forte* and the second *piano*, over a roll for the drum, reminding one, undoubtedly with intention, of the similar ending of the first movement.

Symphony No. 2, in D major, Op. 43

SIBELIUS's Second Symphony, written three years after the First, in 1902, constitutes in many respects a re-

markable advance on the latter. While the First Symphony, one may say, is the archetype of the romantic,
picturesque symphony of the latter part of the nineteenth century, the Second strikes out a new path
altogether. The First is a conclusion, the last of a.
dynasty; the Second is the beginning of a new line,
containing the germs of great and fruitful developments. In outward appearance the Second Symphony
would seem to conform to the traditional four-movement formula of *allegro, andante, scherzo,* and *finale,*
but the internal organization of the movements reveals
many important innovations, amounting at times, and
paiticularly in the first movement, to a veritable
revolution, and to the introduction of an entirely new
principle into symphonic form.

The nature of this innovation can be best described by
saying that whereas in the symphony of Sibelius's im-
mediate predecessors and contemporaries the thematic
material generally consists of definite melodic entities
which propagate by means of the method called by
biologists binary fission, by splitting up and disinte-
grating into several thematic personalities, each bar of
the original organism becoming a theme in the development, in the mature symphonic writing of Sibelius the
method is precisely the opposite—namely, he introduces
thematic fragments and proceeds to unite them in the
development. Instead of presenting definite, clear-cut,
melodic personalities in the exposition, taking them to
pieces, dissecting and analysing them in a development
section, and putting them together again in a recapitulation, which is roughly speaking the method of most
nineteenth-century practitioners of symphonic form,
Sibelius inverts the process, introducing thematic fragments in the exposition, building them up into an

organic whole in the development section, then dissolving and dispersing the material back into its primary constituents in a brief recapitulation. The peculiar strength and attraction of this method of construction consists in the fact that it is the method of nature and of life itself; Sibelius's most characteristic movements are born, develop, and die, like all living things.

The Second Symphony is scored for the same orchestra as its predecessor, except that there is no harp, and no percussion save the customary kettle-drums.

First Movement: *allegretto—poco allegro.*

In the First Symphony, as we have seen, the initial movement is built up on definite first and second subjects; here there are none in the accepted conventional sense of the words. The movement begins with a kind of introduction. Firstly there comes a simple rising figure for the strings alone:

Ex. 14.

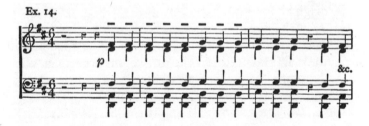

upon which is then superimposed the following pastoral-like theme for wood-wind, punctuated by phrases for the horns echoing in augmentation the final clause of the melody:

Ex. 15.

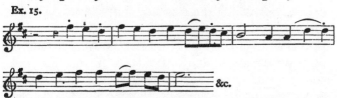

The *tempo* then changes from six-four to common time, and a seemingly somewhat inconsequent episode takes place, initiated by a curious passage for two bassoons in thirds over a roll for the kettle-drums, then a *tremolo* for flutes, then a longish rhapsodical passage for the violins alone.

Ex. 16.

Ex. 17.

Another thematic fragment which occurs in this introduction becomes significant in the course of the movement:

Ex. 18.

An arresting passage for strings *pizzicato* leads to the *allegro*, and to the announcement over the rising string figure with which the movement opened (Example 14) of what would in ordinary parlance, no doubt, be called the 'first subject', for it is probably on the whole the most important one:

Ex. 19.

Flutes. *mf*   *f*

On this its first appearance, however, it seems completely unimportant, and even positively insignificant —merely a perfunctory kind of flourish to accompany the mounting figure in the strings which has already appeared. On its second presentation, however, it already begins to impress itself on one's attention; and when it enters for the third time, at the beginning of what would ordinarily be called the development section, slightly altered, in the minor, for the oboe alone, and is then completed by a pendant for the bassoon:

Ex. 20.

Bassoon.

it seems suddenly to grow in stature before our eyes, or rather, our ears. And so on, with each repetition or variation it develops and expands until in the end it overshadows all.

Nothing, from a purely technical point of view, is more remarkable in the entire range of symphonic literature than the way in which the composer, having presented in the exposition a handful of seemingly dis-

connected and meaningless scraps of melody, proceeds
in the development section to breathe life into them
and bring them into relation with one another. A
further thematic germ, by the way, which plays an
important part in the movement, is the following see-
saw figure which first appears in the introduction and
is modified in the development section into:

Ex. 21.

The formal and emotional apex of the movement is
reached with a particularly imposing twofold statement of the modified version of Example 19 (with
the addition of Example 20), for the strings, followed by
a reference to its original form by the trumpets, then
by a magnificent transfiguration and enhancement for
the full brass of Examples 16 and 17.

The remainder of the movement, as already suggested, consists of a recapitulation in which the
thematic material is resolved back, as it were, into the
elements from which it took rise, yet never with a sense
of anti-climax, but always with a logical inevitability
that holds our attention to the end, which is practically
identical with the beginning—the simple rising figure
for the strings alone. (Example 14.)

Second Movement: *tempo andante, ma rubato—allegro—
andante sostenuto.*

This second movement is also highly individual both
in form and content. The familiar principle of the
contrast between a chief lyrical subject and a more
virile second subject is here intensified into an epic

conflict, involving several groups of thematic protagonists.

It begins with a roll on the kettle-drums, and a long
mysterious *pizzicato* passage shared by basses and
'cellos, over which is eventually given out a melancholy
reflective theme for the bassoons in octaves, continued
by oboes and clarinets:

This is immediately succeeded by a strenuous, restless episode of a somewhat sinister character introducing,
amongst other less important thematic material, the
following pregnant motive which plays a predominant
part in the movement:

This section concludes with sombre, threatening
harmonies for the brass, after which the *tempo* quietens
down, and a second lyrical subject is adumbrated in

the strings, alone at first, and then to a liquid running accompaniment in thirds for flutes and bassoons:

Ex. 24.

This is followed by a sequel of exquisite beauty—one of Sibelius's happiest melodic inventions—for oboe and clarinets:

Ex. 25.

Clarinets and Oboe.

This also generates an angry, threatening reply from the 'cellos and basses, after which a reversion is made to the first subject (Example 22), which is once more driven from the field by an enhanced repetition of the first strenuous passage. The second lyrical subject then recurs and, despite a vigorous attempt on the part of the hostile forces to dislodge it, continues unperturbed on its way. The sequel to this second lyrical subject (Example 25) is then worked up to a passionate and exultant climax, but in this Ormuzd and Ahriman conflict between the forces of light and darkness the latter gain the day and have the last word. The movement closes on a sombre note, with fragmentary references to the two lyrical subjects, and a strange and sinister episode characterized by trills and tremolos for the woodwind, and a furious demi-semiquaver passage for the strings.

Third Movement: *vivacissimo.*

In spite of the indication 'with the utmost vivacity'

and the major tonality (B flat), the mood and general atmosphere of the third movement is restless and uneasy rather than cheerful. The subject-matter of the third movement, unlike its predecessors in this, is decidedly exiguous in quantity, consisting almost entirely in developments and repetitions of the two following motives:

Particular attention should be paid—though no attentive listener or reader is likely to miss it—to the remarkable passage in which the strings discuss and develop Example 26, and the wood-wind Example 27, together with an exceedingly effective and arresting piece of writing for the bass tuba:

The *scherzo* section is followed in orthodox fashion by a *trio, lento e soave*, built on a theme for the oboe of which the poignant loveliness is something of a mystery, seeing that it consists almost entirely of one note, which is repeated no fewer than nine times at the very outset:

Ex. 29.

Both *scherzo* and *trio* are then repeated, not note for note, but so far as thematic substance and general treatment are concerned, and then a tumultuous bridge passage leads directly without a break into the *finale*.

Fourth Movement: *allegro moderato.*

Formally, and in every other sense as well, this is the simplest and most straightforward movement in the symphony, and the least in need of thematic analysis or explanation of any kind. The first chief theme is that with which it starts, for the violins:

Ex. 30.

It is succeeded by several satellites, or continuations —one for the trumpets, another, with an abrupt divagation into B flat, for the horns, and a third for the strings again. The initial clause is once more reverted to, and built up into a more extended melody.

The second main subject is first heard in the wood-wind, over a running figure of accompaniment in the violas and 'cellos:

Ex. 31.
Flute.

Oboe.

Flute.   &c.

A third motive which plays an important part in the proceedings is:

Ex. 32.

&c.

Trombones.

After the thematic material has been thus set forth a kind of working-out section ensues, beginning with alternating references to Examples 30 and 31. The latter then fades out, and the field is left to the first subject and Example 32. These are worked to a climax, culminating in the triumphant restatement of the first section of the movement. The second subject is then resumed and developed at greater length than on the occasion of its first appearance, in a long, exciting *crescendo* in which the theme rises higher and higher with each repetition. The movement concludes with a magnificent peroration for the full orchestra, in which the heavy brass plays the leading part.

Symphony No. 3, in C major, Op. 52

In so far as the hackneyed antithesis of 'classic' and 'romantic' signifies anything at all, it may be said without hesitation that the first two symphonies of Sibelius are essentially romantic works: expressive and colouristic considerations tend to outweigh the element of purely formal design. All the music of Sibelius's first mature period, in fact, up to and including the Second Symphony, may be called romantic in tendency. It is equally true to say that it is all essentially Nordic; one cannot imagine it to have been written by a composer of other than northern provenance.

In the year immediately following the composition of the Second Symphony, however, Sibelius wrote his Violin Concerto, which suddenly betrays a totally new orientation of his genius. What strikes one chiefly about the latter work is its essential classicality, and the same is true of all the other major works which he composed between 1902 and 1911. It is true of the string quartet, for example, which also belongs to this period; it is true of the Third Symphony which was written, or at least completed, in 1908. It is also true to say that in all these works one finds a distinctively southern and even Latin element; one could more easily imagine them to have been written by a Frenchman or an Austrian than by a Scandinavian or a Finn.

In the Third Symphony Sibelius avoids both the dark, sombre, threatening tone-colours which predominate in the First, and the rich, opulent sonorities of the Second, in favour of a quiet and restrained, but none the less bright, colour scheme. The bold formal experiments of the Second are for the time being abandoned, and the method of construction employed is for the most part that of the classical masters. In the first part of the last movement alone do we find traces of the more experimental technique evolved in the earlier work.

The Third Symphony is in three movements only, the central one partaking to a certain extent of the nature of both slow movement and *scherzo*, as its *tempo* indication suggests—*andantino con moto, quasi allegretto*. It is scored for the same orchestra as its predecessor, with the further omission of the bass tuba and the third trumpet; even so, the trumpets and trombones are silent throughout the middle movement, and their employment elsewhere is consistently restrained. In the First and Second Symphonies the wind, and especially the brass, is felt to predominate; in the Third the strings definitely take precedence, in accordance with the classical tradition. The texture of the Third is very much lighter in every way than that of either of its predecessors, the style more sensitive, supple, and discreet. The emotional temper of the work too, is in comparison noticeably restrained; neither the heights nor the depths of feeling are anywhere touched.

First Movement: *allegro moderato*.

The movement starts off at once with the first subject in 'cellos and basses:

Ex. 33.

'Cellos & Basses.

There are two main subsidiaries to this first subject:

Ex. 34.

for the strings, and the following, which takes up the last bar of the foregoing example for its own first phrase, for the wood-wind:

Ex. 35.

This also has a kind of pendant or sequel for the violins, which is of some importance:

Ex. 36.

The second subject, heralded by a powerful anticipation in the horns, clarinets, and oboes, is presented in its authentic form by the 'cellos:

Ex. 37.

A semiquaver figure for the strings, which succeeds the second subject, can hardly be profitably quoted here, for despite the important role which it plays in the movement, it does not possess any definite shape or outline, but is in a perpetual state of transformation— it is enough to say that it is a semiquaver figure—no more precise description can be applied to it. In its unceasing metamorphoses this figure acts as a neutral background against which are projected some of the foregoing thematic personalities.

The lively *tempo* then slackens, and after a suave *cantabile* melody for the violins, which, however, plays no thematic part in the subsequent developments, a very curious passage occurs in which half the first violins and a solo flute discourse in ghostly fashion over a dark, groping figure for double basses alone (no 'cellos).

The shifting, protean, semiquaver figure dominates the development section which ensues, and suggestions of the second subject (Example 37) become gradually more prominent. The music grows quietly but steadily in intensity, the scoring becomes fuller, and a grandiose return is effected to the first theme. The recapitulation runs a regular course, but is succeeded by a lengthy coda which initiates an entirely new line of thought save for the occasional intrusion of Example 36. The practice, by the way, of ending a movement thus with something which seems to bear no discoverable relation to anything which has preceded it is one which grows on Sibelius, and his later symphonies reveal many examples of it. This is perhaps the earliest example of it one finds. The theme on which this coda is based is a passionate *largamente* one for horns and wood-wind. The movement concludes with sonorous chords for the full orchestra.

Second Movement: *andantino con moto, quasi allegretto.*

This is one of the simplest, perhaps the very simplest, of all Sibelius's symphonic movements, and requires little or nothing in the way of descriptive analysis. It consists, indeed, of little else than the ringing of the changes, so to speak, upon a single melodic formula by shifting it up and down on to different degrees of the diatonic scale. This is the theme, given out first by the flutes:

Ex. 38.
Flutes.

The interest of the movement consists chiefly in the resourcefully varied scheme of instrumental colouring which the composer gives to this one theme. The final phrase, incidentally, which is as follows:

Ex. 39.
Clarinet.

becomes detached from the original organism in the course of the movement and plays an independent role.

There are one or two brief interludes of no structural significance save that of affording momentary relief from the all-pervading main theme.

Third Movement: *allegro ma non tanto.*

The first half of this movement, as already observed, is the only part of the symphony which recalls the bold and novel methods foreshadowed in its predecessor, and particularly the first movement. As there, several disjointed and in themselves insignificant little melodic figures are announced at the outset, and gradually welded together into a logical and coherent tissue. Of these fragments the following are the most important:

Ex. 40.
Oboes.

Ex. 41.
Clarinets.

Ex. 42.
Flutes & Clarinets.

Attention should be paid, by the way, to a passage near the beginning, where the theme of the preceding movement is alluded to by flutes and oboes:

Ex. 43. *8va*

Flutes. *mp*

loco.

Oboes. *p*

It plays no subsequent part in the movement, however, and does not in fact reappear again. It cannot therefore be said that the movements are thematically inter-connected, in the strict sense of the words.

A figure first introduced by the horns then gives rise to a kind of background pattern for the strings:

Ex. 44.
Violins.

The second section of the movement consists for the most part, like the preceding movement, in ringing a series of melodic and harmonic changes upon a strongly marked, persistent, rhythmical figure. The first clearly defined form in which it appears, in the violas *divisi*, is as follows:

Ex. 45.
Marcato.

Violas.

It is then confided to the horns and finally to the trum-pets and trombones in augmentation, culminating in a triumphant apotheosis over an *ostinato* figure for the strings. The form of the movement is strictly binary: that is to say, once the big theme of the second part of the movement makes its appearance, none of the thematic material of the earlier section recurs.

Symphony No. 4, in A minor, Op. 63

UNTIL quite recently the accepted view of Sibelius in this country, and probably elsewhere, has been that of a composer. almost exclusively preoccupied with the sombre and gloomy aspects of things. Even for musicians themselves his name has tended to connote the aural equivalents of darkness, winter, storm, cold, night, and so forth—chiefly, one suspects, because the composer happens to belong to a country of which the climatic rigours have been greatly exaggerated by writers in search of local colour. The greater familiarity with his work which has come about within the last few years has helped to dispel this prejudice, and has shown that Sibelius is capable of writing music as gay and light-hearted, as genial and sunny, as any composer. No better example of this could be found than the Third Symphony. At the same time, however, there is justification for the popular view in the fact that much of Sibelius's finest and most characteristic work conforms to it. No better example of this could be found than the Fourth.

It would be difficult, indeed, to imagine a more striking contrast than that which exists between the Third and Fourth Symphonies—so striking, that it is difficult to believe that the same composer could have written both; one only knows that no one else would have been capable of writing either of them. They seem, in fact, to belong to two entirely different worlds and to have nothing in common between them; but each of them, none the less, expresses a definite aspect

of their creator's complex personality, and both are
equally individual utterances in their different ways.
There can be no question, however, as to which is the
more important work of the two. The A minor Symphony represents, together with the Seventh perhaps,
the highest point to which the art of Sibelius has yet
attained.

In the notes to the foregoing symphony it was observed that it belonged to what may justifiably be
called a 'classical' period in the composer's productivity,
which lasted from about 1903 until 1911, the year in
which the Fourth Symphony was composed. With this
work we find a sudden dramatic reversion to what might
be called the more romantic and nordic aspect of his
art and personality, and to a resumption of the structural methods which had been adumbrated in the
Second Symphony, particularly its first movement.

In contradistinction to the bright and cheerful mood
of the Third, the prevailing mood of the Fourth is one
of the deepest tragedy and gloom, while its formal
structure is as elusive and baffling as that of the Third
is simple and easily grasped. In style too, the contrast
is equally striking. In place of the definite, clear-cut,
self-contained themes, the plain diatonic harmonies,
and vigorous elementary rhythms of the earlier work,
we get for the most part tiny, pregnant, thematic
germs only, a harmonic idiom at times so strange and
recondite that it cannot even be defined as atonal, and
a prevalence of twisted, dislocated rhythms and syn-
copations. The scoring is austere and forbidding, and
the thought is so highly concentrated that it demands
an equal degree of concentration in the listener.

The comparative absence of sensuous charm, coupled
with the exacting demands it makes upon the intel-

ligence, have so far prevented this symphony from achieving the popularity of the numbers on either side of it—the genial Third and Fifth. It is probable, however, that in time, and with increasing familiarity, it may come to be appreciated as much as, if not more than, any other of the symphonies by the ordinary listener. As Thomas Hardy wrote fifty years ago, in a famous passage in *The Return of the Native*: 'It is a question if the exclusive reign of orthodox beauty is not approaching its last quarter. The new Vale of Tempe may be a gaunt waste in Thule: human souls may find themselves in closer and closer harmony with external things wearing a sombreness distasteful to our race when it was young. The time seems near, if it has not actually arrived, when the chastened sublimity of a moor, a sea, or a mountain, will be all of nature that is absolutely in keeping with the moods of the more thinking among mankind. And ultimately, to the commonest tourist, spots like Iceland may become what the vineyards and myrtle gardens of South Europe are to him now; and Heidelberg and Baden be passed unheeded as he hastens from the Alps to the sand-dunes of Scheveningen.'

The change forecast by Hardy in this prescient passage has already come about, not only as regards our feeling for nature, but for art as well There are already a few who find greater pleasure in the moor, sea, mountains, sand-dunes if you will, and even gaunt wastes, of the Fourth Symphony of Sibelius, than in the more mellow, opulent, and superficially attractive sound-scapes of other composers; and the chances are that in time the majority will come to feel the same. However that may be, the above quotation may enable the listener and student to enter more sympathetically into the spirit of this music.

First Movement: *tempo molto moderato, quasi adagio.*

The first movement is unusual, if not unique, in being a slow movement, constructed, in broad outline, according to the accepted principles of the classical first-movement formula, with regular exposition, development, and recapitulation sections. As an example of compression and elimination of superfluities it is, perhaps, from a purely technical point of view, without parallel in symphonic literature. The initial four notes merely, embracing a compass of an augmented fourth within the duration of no more than three crotchets, constitute the leading theme and principal thematic germ, not merely of the whole movement but, as will be seen, of the entire symphony:

Ex. 46.

After only five bars a solo 'cello gives out the second subject over a ground-bass for the rest of the 'cellos and the double basses divided and muted, on the alternating notes of E and F sharp:

Ex. 47.

The other strings, also muted, enter in continuation over the same figure in the bass, of which the F sharp eventually gains the upper hand and establishes itself, wrenching the music violently out of the original key into the remote tonality of which it is the tonic, with the statement of an extended variant of the principal theme, or motive rather, in the violins:

Ex. 48.

Violins. *mf*   *ff*

This strenuous passage is chiefly characterized by sombre and menacing harmonies uttered by the heavy brass. The atmosphere then suddenly lightens with a fanfare figure for the horns, suggestive of the sun shining suddenly through a veil of mist, which closes in again momentarily, but lifts once more almost immediately in an episode consisting of variants of the two principal subjects; firstly, of Example 47 in the strings, then of Example 46 in the wood-wind.

This temporary respite from the overshadowing gloom of the opening, which may be said to conclude the exposition section, does not last for long, but is succeeded by a curious unison passage for strings unaccompanied, beginning with a solo 'cello, which knits together in rhapsodic fashion the various sparse fragments of thematic material which have made their appearance in the first part of the movement—just as in a dream the events of the preceding day are merged and distorted:

Ex. 49.

In this example the first phrase, it will be seen, is derived from the second subject, Example 47, and the

last phrase from the extended version of the first subject, Example 48, welded together into a single organism. Then over a tremolo passage for strings, consisting
of a figure based upon the first subject, the wood-wind
give out this strange little fragment, of clearly cognate
origin with the first subject, based, as it is, on the
interval of the augmented fourth:

Ex. 50.

This is eventually transferred to the double basses,
'cellos, and bassoons, while a strange, flickering, little
figure appears in the upper wood-wind, still to the
accompaniment in the strings of the figuration based
upon the principal subject. This development section
concludes with a dramatic confrontation of Example 50
in the wood-wind with Example 48, the latter trans-
posed a minor third higher so that its two phrases are
now in the tonic, A minor and major respectively, with
its first notes identical with Example 46, the first subject in its original form. The key-relationships of this
movement, by the way, despite the superficial appearance of atonality, are exceedingly subtle and at the
same time logical, and are a living proof of the truth
that even the most daring modernity of utterance, as
found in this symphony, is always compatible with
the principles underlying the great symphonic art of
the past.

The whole of the former episode in F sharp is now
recapitulated in the tonic, and the movement concludes as it began, with the first subject or motive, this
time, however, rising up from one group of strings to

another and dying away like a wisp of smoke on a long-held A.

Second Movement: *allegro molto vivace.*

The important part played in the first movement by the interval of the augmented fourth will already have been noticed; the same interval dominates the thematic material of the entire Symphony, although the themes in which it appears are different in each movement. In this way Sibelius succeeds in establishing a unity of mood and thought between the constituent movements of the Symphony without impairing the independence of each of them. The chief feature, it will be noted, of the otherwise somewhat pale and colourless little melody given out at the beginning of the second movement by the oboe over a simple accompaniment in the violas, is this interval:

Ex. 51.

As if to make this clearer, it is followed by a brief dialogue between the oboe and the violins, based almost exclusively on this interval.

The *tempo* then changes to two-four, and a curious passage for strings follows of about forty bars in dactylic metre, entirely in unisons and octaves except for its last few bars. Two of its constituent phrases should be carefully noted, quite apart from the fact that both embody the tell-tale interval of the augmented fourth already alluded to:

Ex. 52.

Violins.

&c.

Ex. 53.

Violins.   &c.

After this has run its course there ensues a passage in the original triple *tempo* consisting, melodically, almost exclusively of augmented fourths, for strings. This is followed by variants and repetitions of the first subject, Example 51, and subsidiary material already heard. Then comes a section marked *doppio piu lento* (twice as slow), which seems at first sight or hearing to have absolutely no relation whatsoever to what has gone before, based upon a theme of which the two clauses are as follows:

Ex. 54.

Oboe. *mf*   *rfz*   Violins.

Ex. 55.

Violas. *p*   *rfz*

But now compare them with the two foregoing examples, 52 and 53, and you will see where they come from.

This dramatic and arresting subject is repeated and worked up to a terrific pitch of intensity, particular emphasis being laid on its final explosive diminished fifth, or augmented fourth. The last bars make a brief reference to the first subject, then to the dactylic rhythm of

the ensuing section, and the movement ends abruptly
with soft F drum-taps, in octaves, alone.

Third Movement: *il tempo largo.*

In a volume of reminiscences concerning his life in
Berlin when he was a fellow student with Sibelius, the
Finnish dramatist Adolf Paul has given a graphic description of the composer's habit and manner of impro-
visation. 'The glasses were filled, and Sibelius sat down
at the piano and improvised, softly, dreamily, feeling
his way. Gradually the wandering ideas crystallized
around a definite conception which took the lead, the
whole developing organically.' And in this third movement one has almost the impression that the composer
is improvising at the orchestra in just the same way that
Paul describes him improvising at the piano: starting
almost at random at first, but gradually defining and
clarifying his thought as he goes on. Beginning with a
few seemingly meaningless little melodic fragments in
the wood-wind, over an accompaniment in the 'cellos
and basses, he gradually builds up, step by step, phrase
by phrase, a magnificent subject of which the following is
the final and definitive, though not the longest, version:

Ex. 56.

Violins.

In all the earlier gropings and searchings one feels
latent and concealed the initial progression of two
superimposed rising fifths.

For the rest, the chief thematic material of the movement consists in an expressive melodic formula of which different variants are discussed by the wood-wind:

Ex. 57.

and with which, after the definitive statement of Example 56, the movement concludes. There is a more than passing resemblance, by the way, in the manner in which both this movement and the first end. Significant, too, is the final phrase of the foregoing example, with the prominent augmented fourth between first note and last. In this connexion also, as well as in another we shall soon see, the following phrase for clarinets and bassoons, which comes immediately after Example 57, should be noted:

Ex. 58.
Clarinet.

Fourth Movement: *allegro*.

The *finale* starts off with a melody for the first violins, of which the first two bars are identical with the last example. One could hardly say, however, on that account, that the two movements are thematically interconnected, for in the first place the phrase in the earlier movement only appears once and has, moreover, no thematic significance; secondly, the subject as it appears in the final movement does not play any important role there even, but does not, in fact, recur at all. (In dealing with the next symphony of the series, the Fifth, we shall have occasion to consider at greater length the whole question of the thematic interrelation of different movements in Sibelius's symphonies.)

The real material of the movement, as opposed to this pseudo-first subject, consists, as usual in Sibelius's later symphonies, and especially in the last movements of them, of tiny little melodic fragments, micro-organisms, which are progressively knit together into a coherent and continuous whole. In this connexion, incidentally, it is exceedingly remarkable to observe how Sibelius pursues the same method of construction in so many movements and so many works, applied to the same kind of material, and yet always succeeds in making something entirely different each time. In this instance the most important of these fragments are as follows:

Ex. 59.

Violas. *rfz*

Ex. 60.

Bell. *mf*

Ex. 61.

Violins. *rfz*

Note in the first of these the ever-present interval of the augmented fourth. After these and other similar thematic germs—some of which can hardly be isolated, in the scientific sense of the word—have been presented,

tossed about from one group of instruments to another,
and linked together, there comes a very striking episode in which fresh material is introduced of a more sustained and clearly defined character, of which this is
perhaps the most complete and, as it were, authorita-
tive version:

Ex. 62.

Violins.

This is succeeded by an impressive passage with
Example 59 in the trumpets, running scales for the
strings, and a bell figure. (In performance, by the way,
this part is generally performed on the glockenspiel
instead of the tubular bells which would seem to be
indicated in the score. It would be interesting to know
if this is approved or condoned by the composer—the
effect is entirely different.)

The rest of the movement consists for the most part
in repetitions and variations of the foregoing material.
The close consists of poignantly expressive passages for
the strings, punctuated by interjections for the wood-
wind, and concluding with quiet, sombre harmonies for
strings alone.

Symphony No. 5, in E flat major, Op. 82

ONCE again the next symphony in the series stands
at the very opposite pole to its predecessor in almost
every respect. In the present example there is no
trace of the brooding gloom and sombre melancholy
which constitute the spiritual key-note of the Fourth;
like the Third, it is a sunny, genial work throughout.

The terseness, economy, and extreme concentration of thought, the reticence and sobriety of style which characterize the former, are not to be found in the Fifth. The form, too, of all its movements is comparatively straightforward, the thematic material more definitely melodic, the harmony diatonic and consonant, the instrumentation rich and sonorous, despite the fact that the orchestra employed in it is precisely the same as that of the two preceding symphonies, except for the addition of a third trumpet. There is still no bass tuba, no harp, no 'extra' instrument of any kind, and no percussion save the ordinary kettle-drums, but the volume and opulence of tone which the composer here elicits from the modest forces at his disposal is truly remarkable.

In the Fourth Symphony there is not a bar that could possibly have been written by any other composer; it is a profoundly personal and subjective utterance from first note to last. In the Fifth, on the contrary, there is not a bar, considered in isolation from its context, that could not have been written by some one else, yet, curiously enough, the effect of the whole is just as completely and absolutely individual, as utterly unlike anything else in music, as the Fourth itself.

The comparative accessibility of the Fifth—it is on the whole probably the most popular and frequently performed of all the seven—is perhaps due in part at least to the fact that it was commissioned by the Finnish government in celebration of the composer's fiftieth birthday. It was written in 1915, and is Sibelius's only important large-scale work which belongs to the war period and even for some years subsequent to the war.

A curious feature of the work is that it is sometimes

spoken of as consisting in three movements, and sometimes in four. This uncertainty derives from the fact
that, firstly, no numerals are prefixed to the various
movements in the score, as is customary, and the first
movement definitely falls into two strongly contrasted
sections in such a way that it is possible to regard them
as two separate movements playing without a break,
like the two last movements of the Second Symphony.
Support for this contention may be found in the fact
that the letters inserted in the score at various intervals
for purposes of rehearsal stop short with N and begin
again with A at the very point where the second section
begins; but this is not conclusive, because if the letter-
ing had continued in the normal way the letter Z would
have been reached before the end of the movement. A
fresh beginning would have had to be made some-
where, in fact, and it was probably decided that the
point chosen for the re-lettering was the most suitable,
as undoubtedly it is.

The composer's views on the point are unfortunately
not known. The present writer can only state his own
personal opinion, which has no other authority behind
it, to the effect that the two sections are in fact one
single, indivisible movement; the reason being that
despite their superficial dissimilarity and independence
of each other the same thematic material is to be found
in both, and this seems to him conclusive. Two separate
movements can certainly be interlinked and played
without a break, as in the Second Symphony, and
retain their separate individualities, so long as the
thematic material is distinct, but surely not when the
thematic material is the same in both. We have even
seen, in the last movement of the Third Symphony, a
case in which there are two definite sections which have

no thematic interdependence whatsoever, but no one has yet suggested that they should be regarded as two separate movements. *A fortiori*, to claim that two sections which not only play consecutively, without a break, but are also thematically connected with each other, are in reality two separate movements, seems to the present writer illogical and indefensible. In the following notes, therefore, the two are treated as one and indissoluble—two contrasted sections of a single movement. But the listener, or reader, may if he likes regard the second of these two sections as a kind of interlinked *scherzo*; it does not matter greatly, and is more a question of terminology than anything else, for the section in question does certainly play the part of a *scherzo* in the work viewed as a whole, whether it is regarded as a self-subsistent formal entity or not. From whichever point of view one looks at it, the procedure at least constitutes a tentative step in the direction of making all the movements of a symphony into a continuous whole—a step eventually effected in the Seventh Symphony.

First Movement: *tempo molto moderato—largamente— allegro moderato—presto.*

The principal thematic germ which recurs throughout the movement is announced at the very outset by the first horn:

Ex. 63.

It is completed and discussed by varying dispositions of wood-wind, introducing, incidentally, a little semiquaver *gruppetto* which is of considerable importance:

Ex. 64.

Oboes. *mf*

This is followed by characteristically Sibelian passages in thirds, also for wood-wind. The whole of this opening section is scored for wood-wind, horns, and drums only. Even after the strings enter for the first time the wood-wind still plays the leading part, and announces the striking second subject in octaves against a pattern of rising repeated notes in the violins and violas:

Ex. 65.

Woodwind.

Sempre dolce. *fz*

A passage of fuller scoring then ensues, introducing a new figure in the strings, of no particular thematic moment, however. The foregoing subject-matter is then developed in orthodox fashion, with the wood-wind again playing the leading role and the strings providing a background. When this has run its course the strings initiate a long passage of chromatic figurations, rising and falling, which again acts as a background against which a solo bassoon, doubled at first by a

clarinet, gives out a poignant, chromatic lament, gradually rising higher and higher. Soft chords for trumpets
and trombones then lead to an exceptionally powerful
development of the second subject, confided this time
to the strings, which have hitherto played only a sub-
ordinate part in the movement. This leads to a sonorous
tutti in which the first subject is prominent on the
trumpets. Then comes the sharp break in the movement to which allusion has already been made; the
long-drawn twelve-eight rhythm gives way to a short,
decisive three-four, the tempo accelerates, new material
is introduced, the mood changes, but the theme heard
at the beginning on the horn—the first subject—remains dominant throughout. The most important
item of fresh thematic material introduced in this
second section of the movement is the following tune
for the trumpet, which is worked out at considerable
length.

Ex. 66.

The movement concludes, however, with a grandiose
peroration based upon the first subject against a tur-
bulent, whirling ground-swell in the strings. In the
last bars the mounting violin figuration consists of the
first four notes of the first subject.

Second Movement: *andante mosso, quasi allegretto.*

The second movement resembles in some respects
that of the Third Symphony, consisting of a series of

variations on a simple theme, or rather, pattern, or
design, of a strongly marked rhythmical character. It
would even be true to say that the theme is actually
a rhythm rather than a melody, for the rhythm remains
constant throughout all the variations and developments, whereas the melodic outlines in which it is
embodied are in a continual state of flux. So much so
is this the case, indeed, that it is difficult to lay one's
finger on what should be considered the definitive form
of the subject.

The movement begins with harmonies for horns,
bassoons, and clarinets, against which the 'cellos, sup-
ported by the violas, both *pizzicato*, give out the first
fragmentary version of the theme:

Ex. 67.

to which the flutes reply:

Ex. 68.

The violins, also *pizzicato*, then present a more extended version of the formulas, with the flutes replying
antiphonally, and so it goes on practically throughout
the movement, with the theme constantly changing
and yet remaining fundamentally the same. The formal
plan is so simple that any kind of analysis of it would be
superfluous; certain minor details, on the other hand,
are of considerable interest. Attention should be paid,
for example, to the striking passage near the beginning,

referred to again near the end, in which the violins
give out changing versions of the subject against
harmonies for the wood-wind and horns, frequently
embodying a piquant semi-tonal clash of the notes C,
C sharp, and D:

Ex. 69.

Flutes. *pp*

&c.

mp
Oboes.

Note also, in two separate variations, the occurrence
of the following figures for the double basses in
octaves:

Ex. 70.
p

Basses.

Ex. 71.
mf

Basses.

Third Movement: *allegro molto.*

The final movement is equally simple in form and
broad outline, though frequently complex in detail.
It begins with one of these long, winding passages
for strings alone which are such a distinctive feature
of Sibelius's symphonic style, especially in his later
period. After the wood-wind have participated in this,

a broad, swinging subject is introduced by the horns, reinforced by the strings (Example 72), which is recognizably identical with Examples 70 and 71.

Ex. 72.
Horns.

poco f e deciso.

&c.

This resemblance, which obviously cannot be a mere coincidence, raises once more, in an acute form, the question concerning the thematic interdependence of the movements in Sibelius's symphonies. Let us briefly consider all the apparent instances of it which we have so far encountered. In the First Symphony the melody with which the first movement begins recurs at the beginning of the last movement; in the Third Symphony, the chief theme of the middle movement is referred to briefly at the beginning of the *finale*; in the Fourth Symphony, apart from the omnipresent interval of the augmented fourth, a phrase which occurs at the end of the third movement is clearly related to the theme with which the last movement starts; and finally, there is the present example. (It is possible that there may be other subtle and unobtrusive instances of the same thing, but if so they have escaped the present writer.) But in all the cases noted above there is one important feature in common. Whenever Sibelius introduces into a movement a theme which has already appeared in another, one always finds that its functional purpose, if it has any, is confined to one or other of the movements, and is not spread indiscriminately over both; either the earlier statement is a mere anticipation which is not followed up until the succeeding movement, or else the later statement is merely an echo, which is similarly without any sequel. In the case of the First and Fourth Symphonies the theme in question does not play any functional role in either movement; in the case of the Third Symphony the allusion in the last movement is only a passing, backward glance; in the present case the foreshadowing of the theme in the *finale* is equally transitory—the double bass figurations do not play any thematic part in the slow movement. In the strict sense of the words, then, it can be said that there is no thematic interconnexion of a real, functional order between the movements in any of Sibelius's symphonies. On the other hand, it is certainly true that the telescoping of first movement proper and *scherzo* in the present work, and the anticipation in the slow movement of an important theme in the *finale*, together impart an appearance of formal unity to the whole work which clearly foreshadows the single-movement form of the Seventh Symphony.

After this broad, swinging theme has been firmly established it becomes a background or accompaniment to another subject which appears in the wood-wind in octaves, doubled by the 'cellos playing on their top string. It consists of two clauses:

Ex. 73.

Woodwind and 'Cellos.

ff coll 8va.

This is succeeded by an episode bearing a close affinity to the first part of the movement, and then by an extended treatment of the first part itself, in which the violins are divided into eight parts. Examples 72 and 73 then recur and are worked up to a magnificent climax built on the former.

Symphony No. 6, in D minor, Op. 104

THE remarkable vogue which the symphonies of Sibelius have recently enjoyed in this country, after a long period of neglect, has not as yet been extended to include the sixth of the series. It was written eleven years ago—in 1924—but one can only recall two or three performances of it during the whole of this period, in London at least. At the same time, while it has not achieved the popularity of the first pair or of the Fifth, neither has it as a rule won from the composer's warmest admirers the esteem with which the Fourth and Seventh are regarded. It falls between the stools, in fact, of the appreciation of the many and the appreciation of the few. The impression which it makes upon one at a first hearing is apt to be somewhat negative. It seems neither to soar to the rapturous heights of the Fifth, nor to plumb the sombre depths of the Fourth; it has neither the breadth and grandeur of the first two, nor the fresh charm and sinewy, athletic grace of the Third. On close acquaintance, however, one gradually discovers in it certain individual qualities which earn for it as secure a place in one's critical estimation as is held by any one of the series. As Mr. Constant Lambert rightly says, in his recently published *Music Ho!*, 'Although at present this fascinating study in half-tones, emotional and orchestral, is overshadowed by the grandeur of No. 5, I feel that future commentators may find its intimate quality more indicative of the true Sibelius, just as many of us feel that Beethoven's fourth and eighth symphonies are more *echt-Beethoven* than the popular odd-number symphonies.'

A dictum of the composer which has been extensively quoted is particularly significant in connexion with the Sixth Symphony. On submitting certain works to the consideration of a German music publisher Sibelius observed that, whereas most other modern composers were engaged in manufacturing cocktails of every hue and description, he offered the public pure cold water. And just as the music of Sibelius stands in relation to the music of most other modern composers, so does the Sixth Symphony stand in relation to his own other works. It is, indeed, the purest and coldest water that has yet flowed from the Sibelian fountain. As has already been suggested, the key-note of the work consists in a sense of serenity and poise, avoiding every kind of extreme, and this characteristic is found in every aspect of it. The composer does not make use of the lavish palette of the modern orchestra, but neither does he here restrict himself to the austere, classical orchestra of most of his symphonies, permitting himself the mild relaxation and luxury of a harp, which he had not employed since the First, and a bass clarinet, which he has not elsewhere employed at all in his symphonies. The colouring, in consequence, is neither opulent nor ascetic, neither bright nor sombre, but in intermediate tones, pearl greys and light browns, softly luminous. Similarly the tempos are neither conspicuously fast nor slow; pianissimos and fortissimos are rare; the full orchestra is hardly used at all in the whole work, but when it is, never for purposes of mere sonority.

This suggestion of balance between extremes is further symbolically reflected in the tonality of the first movement, which is ostensibly that of D minor, but with the B natural, giving the impression of hovering ambiguously between major and minor. This modal atmosphere, unusual in the music of Sibelius, which is almost invariably strongly tonal in character, can also be perceived in the other movements; it is a characteristic, indeed, which imparts an underlying spiritual unity to the whole four movements, just as the perpetually recurring interval of the augmented fourth does in the Fourth Symphony, as we have already seen. On the other hand, there is not, so far as the present writer is aware, any instance in this work of a theme from one movement occurring, however fleetingly, in another movement, although this all-pervasive modality might seem to suggest some kind of thematic interconnexion at times.

Altogether, curiously enough, and not merely on account of this modal feeling, the composer of whom one finds oneself thinking most frequently in connexion with this work is Palestrina; and, it is interesting and significant to note, the fact was elicited in an interview with Sibelius which appeared recently in an American musical journal that, apart from Mozart, Palestrina is the composer for whom he has at present the greatest admiration.

First Movement: *allegro molto moderato.*

No better illustration of what has been said above could possibly be found than the opening bars of the whole work. If one were asked to suggest the quietest, most unobtrusive and unassuming way of starting a symphonic movement, one could not think of any one more so than this; a *tempo* neither fast nor slow, but *moderato*; the harmonic interval of a major third, played neither high nor low, by second violins *divisi*, not loudly or softly, but *mezzo forte.* And certainly nothing could be more Palestrinian than the whole of this opening section, not merely by virtue of its modal atmosphere, but also on account of the very style of writing, with its prevalence of conjunct motion, and the diatonic purity, simplicity, and smoothness of the polyphony.

Out of this harmonic background for the strings alone there eventually emerges in the wood-wind a theme of which the first two and most important clauses are as follows:

Ex. 74.
Oboes.

The theme in its full form, as so often with Sibelius, does not appear until later in the movement. (The continuation of these two phrases, on their first appearance, is of no ultimate thematic significance and need not, therefore, be quoted here.)

This section comes to a close with sustained chords for the divided strings on the notes C sharp, E, G, and B, with the common chord of C major in the brass— a curious harmonic effect.

A noteworthy characteristic in all Sibelius's mature symphonic writing is his fondness for little wisps of thematic material consisting of passages of thirds for the wood-wind. Here we encounter a very typical example. It would be difficult to imagine any sequence of notes more unpromising at first sight as a subject for fertile symphonic development than this, presented by the flutes against a simple accompaniment of chords for the harp and repeated notes for the strings:

Ex. 75.
Flutes.

poco f

but it suits Sibelius's purpose. A method of development which he favours in his later symphonies, especially in this one, and more especially in this particular movement of it, may be roughly defined as follows. Suppose a theme to consist of several separate little phrases or recognizable features, *a*, *b*, *c*, and *d*. After introducing it Sibelius will, on repetition, omit *a*, let us say, and substitute for it a new phrase *e*; and so on, gradually, unobtrusively, almost imperceptibly, until eventually one has a theme *e*, *f*, *g*, *h* which, when one refers it back, is found to be entirely different from what one started with. In the same way, in fact—or so we are told—that no single cell of one's body remains the same after seven years, and we are therefore entirely different people at the end of this period from what we were at the beginning of it, although the continuity of personality remains, so the thematic tissue of Sibelius's later style of symphonic writing similarly undergoes a ceaseless process of elimination and replacement, ever renewing, yet always preserving, the same fundamental unity and identity.

For this peculiarly organic method of construction the most suitable material is obviously that of the kind just quoted, permitting as it does the replacement of

one cell by another similar one in such a way that there
is no break in the identity of the whole. Here are a few
of the successive stages through which Example 75
passes in the course of the movement:

Ex. 76.
Violins.

Ex. 77.
Violins.

Ex. 78.
Flutes.

Ex. 79.
Oboes.

Now compare Example 79 with 75, and it will be
seen that they possess no melodic particle in common,
yet there is no break in the organic tissue and continuity of thematic personality. The whole movement
is full of subtleties similar to this. For instance, this
little phrase for the violas:

Ex. 80. Violas.

which is unobtrusively introduced into the midst of the foregoing transformations, is obviously a reference to the first phrase of the principal subject (Example 74). Similarly, this phrase for the violins:

Ex. 81. Violins.

is self-evidently a development of the second phrase of the same example, the last bar, however, consisting of one of the new melodic units which has in the meanwhile been introduced. On top of this latter, again, in the wood-wind, is superimposed another new cell which plays a considerable part:

Ex. 82.
Oboe.

A further thematic personality, of larger dimensions this time, which plays an important role in the movement, is as follows:

Ex. 83.
Violins.

Example 81 is subjected to extensive treatment in various modifications, and eventually becomes a kind of pattern background against which is presented a version of the original theme itself, from which it derives, on the 'cellos, preceded by an anticipation on the bass clarinet. (This, incidentally, is practically the only place in the score in which one is conscious of the presence of this instrument. For the most part it merely performs the unobtrusive function on occasion, when necessary or desirable, of reinforcing the other bass instruments. Similarly, the writing for the harp, that other intruder into the strictly classical symphonic orchestra, is of unexampled moderation and restraint, being almost exclusively limited to the simplest chords and arpeggios.)

A full statement of the principal theme, again by the 'cellos, follows. This is succeeded by one of the more fully scored and sonorous passages in the movement, with brilliant figurations for violins and wood-wind. The heavy brass, however, remains practically silent throughout the movement, from near the beginning till right at the end.

The close of the movement is abrupt and somewhat enigmatic. Its hitherto even and placid course is suddenly interrupted by dark, threatening, *tremolo* harmonies for 'cellos and double basses *divisi*, occurring three times, after which the more important thematic material is briefly passed in review in exceedingly concentrated and compressed form. A flaring *fortissimo* chord for the brass in C major, as at the beginning, emphasizes the tonal ambiguity which is such a prominent feature of the movement, and a quiet close follows with references to the main subject. (Note the inconclusive modal cadence.)

Second Movement: *allegretto moderato.*

As the *tempo* indication implies, this is not, strictly

speaking, a slow movement, though it performs the function of one with regard to the work as a whole. The form, like that of the orthodox slow movement, is lyrical, and occupied primarily with the restatement and development of one idea, rather than in the opposition or interaction of two or more.

The movement begins with a subtle and ingenious effect of syncopation—chords for flutes and bassoons seemingly in six-eight rhythm, but actually in three-four cross rhythms, as appears after eight bars, when the chords dissolve into an ordinary three-four, with a delightful little jar:

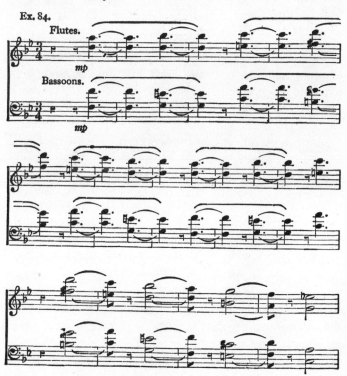

Ex. 84.

Eventually in front of this background of wood-wind chords is set a curiously attractive, wayward, gracefully indolent melody which the first and second violins throw like a ball from one to the other:

Ex. 85. Violins.

mp espress.

This subject is treated and repeated at greater length than is customary in the later Sibelius, at first with extreme economy of instrumentation and later with fuller scoring. It is, strictly speaking, the only thematic material in the movement. After its presentation and repetition there is an abrupt break, and the instrumental roles are reversed, with the strings constituting a background of a typically Sibelian kind against which the wood-wind give out little fragmentary interjections which gradually become longer and more sharply defined; but they never become sufficiently so to constitute quotable themes.

The whole of this section, by the way, is perhaps the only passage in all the music of Sibelius which recalls Wagner—the *Waldweben* in 'Siegfried'. But the resemblance is purely superficial, consisting merely in the fact that both are forest music, full of the rustling of leaves and the songs of birds. The forest of Wagner is recognizably a Teutonic one—the Hercynian forest of Tacitus—and the birds in it sing with the voices of human beings—it is essentially anthropomorphic nature music. The forest of Sibelius, on the other hand, is a far northern one, of spruce, birch, and alder, less luxuriant in foliage, and the bird songs are those of Nature herself, bearing no resemblance to the music of man, and conveying no message save that of their living loveliness.

Instead of returning to the first part of the movement, as one naturally expects him to do, and repeating it integrally as most other composers would, Sibelius concludes with merely a few bars of oblique and perfunctory reference to it for the sake of formal cohesion. He has already said all he had to say on the subject, and disdains mere mechanical repetition.

Third Movement: *poco vivace.*

This is a typical *scherzo* movement, except for the fact that it is all of a piece, and has no contrasting *trio* section. It is short in comparison with the other movements and is built up almost entirely out of the theme in trochaic metre with which the movement opens, in the strings:

Ex. 86.

Violins.

and the easily recognizable sequel which follows immediately after in the wood-wind:

Ex. 87.

All is perfectly simple and straightforward, standing in no need of comment, explanation, or analysis. The scoring is, on the whole, noticeably fuller than that of the preceding movements, but none the less always restrained, save perhaps for a sudden Haydnesque ejaculation—*sforzando*—for trumpets and trombones which twice interrupts the otherwise even tenor of the music.

Fourth Movement: *allegro molto.*

The *tempo* indication *allegro molto*, as applied to the beginning of the movement, is somewhat misleading; conductors are apt to take the first bars much too fast and, in consequence, to make them sound utterly ridiculous.

The principal subject, as so often in Sibelius's final movements, is characterized by a sharply defined and easily recognizable rhythm, here encountered in the very first bar:

Ex. 88.
Violins.

The subsidiary material out of which the movement is built again, as so often, consists of a multiplicity of small motives of which the most important, certainly the most arresting, is as follows:

The characteristic rhythm of the first bars of the chief subject, however, dominates the movement throughout, appearing sometimes in the most unlikely melodic guises, and never long absent from the scene. In the following passage, for example, it is obviously referred to in diminution:

In the concluding section of the movement the subject itself undergoes a process of enlargement and enhancement as the culminating clause of a larger whole, twenty bars long, of which the first part is built up on the rhythm already mentioned:

Ex. 91.

Violins.

&c.

After this has run its course the vigour and vitality suddenly ebb from the music. The time-signature becomes *doppio piu lento*—twice as slow—the foregoing melodic material disappears entirely, and the work ends with what appears to be an entirely fresh line of thought, bearing no relation to anything that has gone before. In spite of this apparent formal *non sequitur* there is something curiously satisfying in this unexpected ending, like a quiet, serene evening after a boisterous day. The writing for the strings in these final pages is of a loveliness rare even in Sibelius, who excels in such moments. There is something positively uncanny in these magical sounds. On paper there is nothing there; it is all perfectly simple and straightforward. But in performance it is like nothing else in all music except his own.

The very last bars give a curious sense of infinity, tapering into silence in the same way that the long, level vista of the countless islands, lakes, and forests of the Finnish landscape merges into the far horizon.

Symphony No. 7, in C major, Op. 105

SYMPHONIES in general, it may have been noticed, consist of four movements, but there have always been exceptions to what was never anything more than a convention. Formerly such exceptions tended in the direction of augmentation rather than of diminution in the usual number. Berlioz's 'Symphonie fantastique' is in five movements, and the record is probably held by Anton Rubinstein in his 'Ocean Symphony', with one movement for each of the Seven Seas. In more recent times, however, composers have shown a marked predilection for triptych form, generally with a slow movement between two fast ones, and Sibelius, as we have seen, has adopted this plan in his Third and Fifth. Apart from Liszt's 'Dante' Symphony, on the other hand, it is difficult to think of any complete symphony in two movements only, and even this exception is better regarded as a symphonic poem in two movements, which is a very different thing from a symphony. Sibelius's Seventh is probably the only example there is of a symphony of any importance which consists only of one movement.

In spite of the fact that it is in one movement only, there is no symphony in the literature of music which conforms more closely with all the demands and conditions of the form; in the opinion of a steadily increasing number of people it is considered to be one of the most masterly and impressive examples of the form in existence.

The looseness with which the expressions 'symphony' and 'symphonic' are employed by writers on music has been productive of much confusion of thought. No better exemplification of what constitutes the essence of symphonic writing could be found than that which is afforded by a comparison between this symphony and the symphonic poem 'Tapiola', written by Sibelius in precisely the same year—1925. The crucial difference is not that one is to some extent based upon some extraneous poetic idea while the other is not, but that the symphonic poem is mono-thematic, whereas the symphony is poly-thematic; in other words, the musical texture of 'Tapiola' is entirely evolved from one melodic germ, whereas that of the symphony is evolved from the interaction of many melodic germs.

Apart from that, however, the whole style and conception are entirely different, yet one finds critics saying that 'Tapiola' is one of the finest examples of 'symphonic writing' in music: the truth being that it constitutes the best example one could possibly find of a work exemplifying precisely the opposite ideal from that implied in the word 'symphonic'.

The essence of the symphony, considered as a form or style, consists in multiplicity and diversity, both of mood and of subject-matter: that of the symphonic poem in homogeneity and unity of both. The problem in writing a symphonic poem is, how to impart diversity and variety of treatment to a unity of subject-matter; the problem in writing a symphony is, how to impart unity of design to a variety and diversity of subject-matter, and the crux of the problem lies in the relation which exists, or should exist, between the various constituent movements. In the old classical symphony one finds only too often that the four movements bear no relation to each other at all; each of them might just as well belong to any other symphony. In the romantic symphony of the nineteenth century one finds only too often precisely the contrary fault, that of a too close connexion between the various movements produced by the recurrence of a theme or themes in one movement which has or have already played a part in a preceding movement. It is a matter of common observation, for example, that with 'the triumphant return of the motto theme' in the last movement, which so monotonously characterizes the symphonies of this school, the formal interest of the work invariably and inevitably collapses into a rhetorical blancmange.

Sibelius never falls into this error; as we have seen in preceding examples, whenever a theme from one movement recurs momentarily in another in his symphonies, its function is always restricted to one or other of the movements. At the same time, however, he avoids the fault of so many classical symphonies; he is always deeply concerned to establish an underlying spiritual relationship between the separate movements, while jealously preserving their identity and independence.

In the Seventh Symphony his solution of the eternal problem of the form has been to make it in one gigantic movement which, at the same time, consists of four definite sections. Firstly, there comes a slow introductory section, then a moderately fast one, then a section which is clearly akin to a *scherzo*, and lastly, a broad, monumental *finale*. But while thus preserving in broad outline the four-movement convention, the work viewed as a whole reveals the presence of the formal principle exemplified in orthodox sonata form —the triune symmetry of exposition, development, and recapitulation. In the slow introduction the chief thematic protagonists make their appearance; in the following section they are worked out; in the *scherzo*-like episode fresh material is introduced, but development is still continued; and the final peroration is clearly in the nature of a recapitulation. The resultant form. therefore, is not merely one of four interlinked movements, but constitutes a single and indissoluble organism at the same time. In this respect the Seventh Symphony of Sibelius is, from a purely abstract and objective point of view, unique.

The symphony begins with a soft drum-tap, followed

by a simple, rising scale passage for strings, first in the 'cellos and double-basses, and then in all. The cloudy, dissonant chord with which it concludes resolves itself into an F major common chord, over which the flute announce the following phrase:

Ex. 92.

This is repeated a tone lower by the clarinets, then in a rhythmically modified form by the flutes again, and this also is echoed by the clarinets. In the succeeding bar the first violins give out this fragment:

Ex. 93.

Two more short, fragmentary ideas of lesser thematic import then appear, one in dialogue between strings and wood-wind, and the other in the flutes and clarinets, concluding with a short descending scale passage for flute and bassoon.

In striking contrast with the foregoing disjointed and seemingly haphazard statements is the succeeding broad, sustained passage for divided strings alone, beginning in the violas and 'cellos. The other strings are gradually added, and then the wood-wind; after which a climax, not so much of tonal volume as of emotive and structural intensity, is reached with the presentation of the following imposing subject by a solo trombone:

Ex. 94.

mf sonore.

&c.

This is also succeeded by two or three less important thematic fragments which nevertheless play a considerable role at the close of the work, and should therefore be noted:

Ex. 95.
Flutes and Clarinets.

mf

&c.

Ex. 96.
'Cellos and Basses.

mp   *mf*   *poco f*   &c.

Ex. 97.
Flute.

mf

This concludes the section which has been described above as corresponding roughly with the exposition section of the classical symphonic form. The chief thematic protagonists of the subsequent developments are all there, the most important being Example 93 and the big trombone theme, Example 94, the former chiefly characterized by the interval of a semitone rising to the

tonic, the latter by the interval of a whole tone descending to the tonic.

The section which has been compared to the development section of the ordinary symphonic movement
begins with the recurrence of the rising scale passage of
the opening bars of the work, continued, firstly by the
addition of Example 92, and secondly by that of
Example 93—a kind of dovetailing which is highly
typical of the composer, and a method of construction
which is to be found in practically all his symphonies.
The tempo quickens, and a short, strenuous passage
concludes with a phrase in which the characteristic progression of the trombone theme in the horns is heard
against Example 90, with its characteristic rising semitone:

Ex. 98.

The intricate developments which follow are largely
dominated by thematic germs embodying this rising
semitone. One modification which plays an important
part is this:

Ex. 99.

The intricate developments which follow are largely
dominated by thematic germs embodying this rising
semitone. One modification which plays an important
part is this:

On the other hand, a pregnant little figure which
does not appear to be derived from, or related to, any of

the foregoing material, makes a dramatic appearance in
the strings:

Ex. 100.

1st Violins.

With the advent of the latter on the scene the steadily increasing velocity of the tempo reaches a *vivacissimo*, which leads to a strenuous restatement of the
trombone theme in the minor over a chromatic ground-
swell in the strings. After this impressive episode has
run its course, the powerful tragic mood it has generated
almost imperceptibly lightens, and the sombre harmonies are gradually infiltrated with light in a masterly
transition passage which leads into the gay *scherzo-
like* section.

This part of the movement, as already observed, introduces much fresh material, the most important
elements of which are the following:

Ex. 101.

Woodwind. Horn *8va bassa.*

Ex. 102.

1st Violins.

Ex. 103.

Oboe. 1st Violins.

Particularly remarkable is the way in which these and other thematic fragments are here varied, developed, and juxtaposed, forming a continuous and homogeneous texture. One of these others, by the way, is of great significance, combining as it does the two typical features of the two principal protagonists of the work—the falling super-tonic, and the rising leading-note:

Ex. 104.

2nd Flute.

As the *scherzo* episode progresses Example 101 seems continually to grow in size, and eventually dominates everything else, whereupon the tempo quickens to *vivace*, and another transition passage leads into the final section of the symphony. From here onwards to the end all is plain sailing, the chief feature being a grandiose restatement of the big trombone theme, heralded by one of those tumultuous string passages which are so typical of the composer, and of which he alone seems to possess the secret. As in the corresponding first section of the movement, the presentation of the trombone theme is succeeded by that of Examples 95, 96, and 97. The latter in particular, delivered triple *forte largamente* by the strings alone, achieves a veritable apotheosis.

The work comes to a tranquil close with a fragmentary reference to Example 94 in horns and bassoons, a more extended discussion of Example 92 in its modified form over tremolos in the strings, and a harmonic progression for the latter instruments virtually identical, curiously enough, with one in 'Valse triste', of all things, magically transmuted, however:

Ex. 105.

Ex. 106.
'Valse triste.'

Finally, in the last bars, are presented the two simple, melodic progressions which underlie the entire work: firstly, the super-tonic falling to the tonic, then the leading-note rising to it—constituting a kind of triumphal Q.E.D. to the whole proposition put forward at the outset.

Ex. 107.
Tempo I.